FLOWERS, FRUITS AND SEEDS

Angela Royston

Heinemann LIBRARY

Making new plants

Most kinds of plants produce **flowers** every year. How many different colours can you see in these flowers? Some have more than one colour.

Different kinds of flowers have different shapes and numbers of petals, but the job of all flowers is to make **seeds** which will grow into new plants.

Buds

A flower begins as a **bud** growing on the end of a **stem**. While the bud is closed, it is protected by green **sepals**.

As the bud grows bigger, the sepals
slowly unfold. The bud unfolds too
and opens up into a **flower**.

Male and female flowers

Some plants have two kinds of
flowers. These catkins are the male
flowers of the hazel tree. They make
lots of tiny grains of **pollen**.

The hazel's female flower is small and hard to spot. Inside the red tips are tiny flower-eggs called **ovules**.

Grass flowers

Grass has green **flowers** which produce both male **pollen** and female **ovules**.

The wind blows pollen from one flower onto another flower. When a grain of pollen joins with an ovule, the ovule becomes a **fertilized seed**.

Colourful flowers

Many colourful **flowers** have both male and female parts. The male **anthers** are covered with **pollen**. In the middle of the anthers is the female **style**.

Brightly coloured flowers often have a sweet smell. Their colour and scent attract insects which come to feed on a sweet juice called **nectar**.

Birds and bees

Can you see the **pollen** sticking to this bee? Some grains of pollen will rub off onto the **style** of the next **flower** it visits.

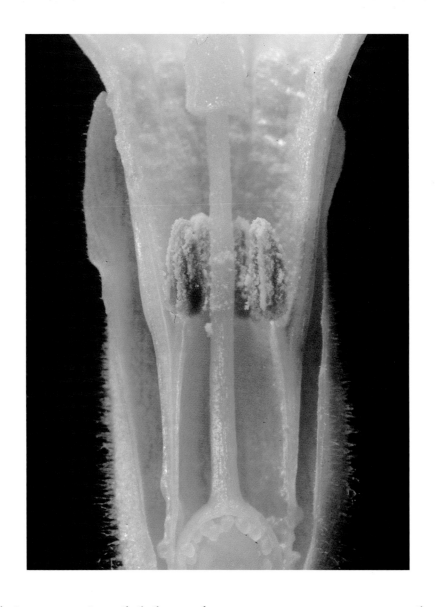

This marigold has been cut open to show the **ovules** at the bottom of the style. Pollen from another marigold passes down the style to **fertilize** the ovules.

Ripening seeds

When the **ovules** are **fertilized**, the petals wither and die. Can you see wilted flowers on this cherry tree? The cherry **seeds** are beginning to swell.

A juicy **fruit** grows around the seeds to protect them. These cherries are now ripe and ready to eat.

Juicy fruits

Can you see the **seeds** inside this
kiwi **fruit**? Seeds grow best if they are
scattered far from the parent plant.
Birds help to scatter some seeds.

When a bird feeds on fruit and berries, the seeds pass through its body. If a seed falls on to good soil, it may start to grow into a new plant.

Blown by the wind

Many **seeds** are scattered by the wind.
The seeds of some trees have wings to
help them blow further.

Dandelion seeds have little parachutes which help them float a long way through the air before they land.

Pods

The **seeds** of peas, beans, lupins and many other plants grow inside pods. As the seeds swell, the pods grow longer and fatter.

When the seeds are ripe, the pod splits and the seeds are catapulted onto fresh ground away from the parent plant.

Nuts

A nut is a **seed** inside a hard shell. Mice and other animals bury a store of nuts in the ground. Some of them grow into new plants.

Coconuts grow on palm trees on the beach. Some of the nuts float across the sea to other islands and start to grow there.

A new plant

Most **seeds** do not grow into plants,
but this seed has fallen on good soil.
It lies in the soil until the weather is
warm enough for it to grow.

It may wait until the following spring before it begins to grow into a new plant. First the **root** grows, then a shoot.

Watch it grow

Plant some **seeds** and watch them grow into **flowers**! Use sunflower seeds from the supermarket. Soak them in water for a day and then plant each in a pot of damp soil.

Once the seeds have started to grow, water the pot every few days. How tall does your sunflower grow? Look for new seeds when the flower dies.

Plant map

a strawberry plant

leaf

flower

fruit

stem

roots

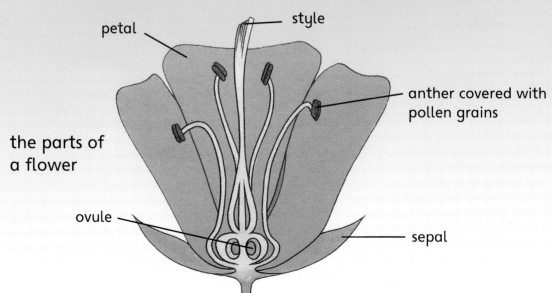

the parts of a flower

petal

style

anther covered with pollen grains

ovule

sepal